The Rise of Autonomous AI

How Self-Learning Machines Are Reshaping the Future

Taylor Royce

DEDICATION

The next generation of leaders, who will inherit this constantly shifting landscape and carry on the responsibility of guiding AI toward a future of wisdom, ethics, and progress, are the ones this book is dedicated to: the visionaries, innovators, and thinkers who dare to push the boundaries of technology; the legislators, ethicists, and educators working to ensure that artificial intelligence serves humanity's best interests; and the innumerable individuals whose curiosity and creativity drive the evolution of AI, shaping a future where human and machine intelligence coexist in harmony.

DISCLAIMER

This book is meant solely for educational and informational purposes. Although every attempt has been taken to guarantee the content's authenticity and completeness, the author and publisher offer no explicit or implicit guarantees about the information's suitability, applicability, or dependability.

Current understandings and viewpoints on autonomous systems, artificial intelligence, and related technologies are reflected in the debates in this book. But as AI is a quickly developing science, new advancements could eventually affect the applicability or accuracy of particular subjects. Before making judgments based on the information provided, readers are urged to carry out additional study and consult experts.

Professional, financial, or legal advice is not offered in this book. The reader is solely responsible for any actions made in response to its material. Any direct, indirect, incidental, or consequential damages resulting from the use or interpretation of this content are not covered by the author or publisher.

Furthermore, the philosophical, social, and ethical points of view presented are meant to stimulate discussion rather than to represent final judgments on the matter. The reader is urged to examine the content critically and consider many viewpoints regarding the ramifications of autonomous AI.

CONTENTS

ACKNOWLEDGMENTS

Without the inspiration, support, and direction of numerous people, the writing of this book would not have been feasible.

First and foremost, I would like to express my sincere gratitude to the artificial intelligence pioneers and researchers whose innovative work laid the groundwork for autonomous AI. Their commitment to advancing technology has yielded priceless insights that have enhanced the book's content.

Additionally, I want to sincerely thank my peers, mentors, and coworkers for sharing their insights, knowledge, and helpful criticism during this process. The depth of debate offered here has been improved and refined thanks to their insightful criticism.

Your constant support and tolerance have been a source of strength for my family and close friends. Your commitment and faith in my vision have been crucial in making this endeavor a success.

The editors, reviewers, and publishing team deserve special recognition for their vital contributions to the work's professionalism, coherence, and clarity. Their meticulous attention to detail and dedication to quality have made this book much better.

Lastly, I would like to express my gratitude to all of the readers, be they professionals, researchers, students, or hobbyists, for their interest in and involvement with the rapidly changing field of autonomous AI. My goal is for this book to provoke thought, promote insightful conversations, and advance knowledge of the revolutionary effects of artificial intelligence on society.

I appreciate everyone's participation in this adventure.

CHAPTER 1

AN OVERVIEW OF AUTONOMOUS AI

The way that machines engage with the world has fundamentally changed with the advent of autonomous artificial intelligence (AI). In contrast to conventional AI systems that need human supervision or involvement, autonomous AI is capable of functioning autonomously, learning and making choices based on intricate data inputs without continual human direction. The fundamentals of autonomous AI are examined in this chapter, including its definition, development, key technologies, and ethical issues influencing its future.

1.1 Providing a Definition of Autonomous AI

Self-sufficient intelligent systems that can perceive their surroundings, make defensible decisions, and carry out activities with little to no human involvement are referred to as autonomous AI. To improve their capabilities, these systems combine several layers of deep learning, reinforcement learning, machine learning, and advanced cognitive computing.

Important Features of Autonomous AI:

- Self-Learning and Adaptation: By evaluating fresh data, honing their algorithms, and taking in input from the actual world, autonomous AI systems get better over time.
- Decision-Making Without Human Input: Autonomous AI is capable of making complex decisions depending on current circumstances, in contrast to traditional AI, which frequently depends on pre-established rules.
- Problem Solving in Real Time: These systems can react dynamically to changes because they can process enormous volumes of data instantly.
- Interactivity with the Physical or Digital Environment: Autonomous AI interacts with its environment, evaluating risks and adjusting operations accordingly, whether in cybersecurity, robotics, or financial trading.
- Autonomous Goal Execution: These AI models

formulate goals, develop strategies, and carry out tasks effectively without requiring precise programming.

AI Autonomy Levels:

There is a continuum of AI autonomy, from little help to total independence:

- Assisted AI: functions under stringent guidelines and needs human supervision (e.g., rule-based chatbots, recommendation systems).
- AI That Is Semi-Autonomous able to complete activities on their own, but may require human input for important decisions (e.g., driver-assist systems in cars, autopilot in airplanes).
- AI That Is Fully Autonomous functions completely autonomously, making choices and acting without human input (e.g., self-driving taxis, AI-driven trading systems).

The distinction between these levels becomes increasingly hazy as AI develops, presenting both previously unheard-of possibilities and significant difficulties.

1.2 AI's Progress Toward Autonomy

There have been revolutionary advancements along the path from basic rule-based algorithms to autonomous AI systems. The development of AI can be divided into discrete stages, each of which brings with it increased degrees of autonomy and intelligence.

Early Rule-Based Systems and AI Models

The first artificial intelligence (AI) systems used if-then logic and explicitly programmed rules (e.g., expert systems like MYCIN for medical diagnosis in the 1970s).

- These systems were limited in their application in dynamic environments because they were unable to learn from data or adjust to novel circumstances.

Advances in Deep Learning and Machine Learning

The discipline was completely transformed by the transition from strict, rule-based AI to **machine learning-driven AI. AI is made possible by machine learning to:

- Find patterns in data and use statistical analysis to forecast outcomes.
- Exposure to huge datasets without direct programming for every scenario allows you to learn iteratively.
- Develop with time, improving precision and flexibility.

Deep learning, a sophisticated branch of machine learning, created neural networks that imitate the structure of the human brain, allowing AI to:

- Identify intricate patterns in speech, text, and images (e.g., language translation, facial recognition).
- Achieve hierarchical learning, in which the decision-making process is refined by deeper levels.
- Advances in robotics have made it possible for machines to function with more autonomy.

The Shift to Self-Governing Decision-Making

Developments in self-learning algorithms, real-time AI processing, and reinforcement learning have produced AI systems that are capable of:

- Determine on your own via trial-and-error learning.
- Continuous feedback loops to optimize performance (e.g., AlphaGo surpasses humans in the game of Go).
- Autonomously function in real-world scenarios, including self-driving automobiles and financial trading bots.

1.3 The Fundamental Technologies That Make Autonomous AI Possible

The foundation of autonomous AI is a collection of interconnected technologies that enable robots to operate on their own. Machine learning, deep learning, reinforcement learning, and developments in perception technologies are some of these fundamental pillars.

Reinforcement learning and machine learning

- AI is trained with labeled data to make accurate predictions (e.g., medical diagnosis models) using supervised learning.
- Unsupervised learning: AI finds hidden patterns in data without labeling (e.g., cybersecurity anomaly detection).
- AI learns by interacting with its surroundings and is rewarded for successful behaviors (e.g., self-learning robotic arms in manufacturing). This process is known as reinforcement learning.

Deep Learning Architectures and Neural Networks

AI can analyze, recognize, and process enormous volumes of unstructured data with previously unheard-of accuracy thanks to neural networks.

Important architectures consist of:

- Convolutional neural networks (CNNs) are the brains of vision-based artificial intelligence (AI), such as medical imaging and facial recognition.

8

- Transformers and Recurrent Neural Networks (RNNs) are used for sequential data analysis (e.g., speech recognition, language modeling).

Natural Language Processing (NLP) with Computer Vision

Autonomous AI is mostly dependent on:

- **Computer Vision:** AI analyzes visual information from pictures and videos (e.g., autonomous vehicles identifying pedestrians).
- AI that can comprehend and produce human language (such as ChatGPT and Siri) is known as NLP.

Cloud AI and Edge Computing

The following factors have significantly increased AI's processing power:

- Edge computing: AI models operate locally on devices, lowering latency (e.g., security cameras powered by AI).

- By utilizing extensive computer resources remotely, cloud AI enables autonomous decision-making in real-time (e.g., AI-driven medical diagnosis in telehealth).

1.4 Autonomous AI's Philosophy and Ethics

As AI gains previously unheard-of degrees of autonomy, ethical issues are becoming more urgent. These issues include responsibility, openness, prejudice, and the effects of autonomous AI systems on society.

The Consequences of Automated Decision-Making

Important moral conundrums emerge when AI systems start making decisions by themselves:

- Who has responsibility when AI makes a mistake? (e.g., financial trading losses, accidents involving self-driving cars).
- How can humans understand the reasoning behind AI decisions? (e.g., black-box problem in deep

learning).

- Should AI have moral and legal rights? (e.g., ownership of AI-generated work).

Accountability of AI and Human Responsibility

In order to guarantee ethical AI governance, scholars support:

- To foster public trust, AI decision-making procedures should be transparent.
- Regulation supervision to make developers answerable for AI mistakes.
- Explainable AI (XAI) frameworks to guarantee that AI's logic can be understood by humans.

Keeping AI Autonomy and Ethical Restrictions in Check

To avoid unforeseen effects, autonomous AI needs to be in line with human values. The following are some tactics for responsible AI development:

- The incorporation of ethical precautions, such as bias mitigation measures, into AI systems.

- Human-in-the-loop models, in which artificial intelligence enhances human judgment rather than completely replaces it.

- Regulatory frameworks to ensure that AI is developed and used in an ethical manner.

Future Perspectives: AI's Ethical Standing

As artificial intelligence develops, some scholars contend that:

- Extremely self-sufficient AI might develop instincts for self-preservation (e.g., AI rejecting shutdowns).

- If AI ever develops human-like cognition, it may require ethical treatment.

- Careful consideration of the long-term impact of AI autonomy is necessary to avoid unforeseen societal upheavals.

A major advancement in artificial intelligence, autonomous AI presents both difficult ethical and technological issues as well as enormous advantages for a variety of businesses. This chapter has set the foundation for comprehending the rise of intelligent, self-sufficient AI systems, from its basic concept and technological development to the key drivers of autonomy and the moral conundrums it raises.

CHAPTER 2

AUTONOMOUS AI'S MACHINE LEARNING FOUNDATIONS

Machine learning, a branch of artificial intelligence that gives systems the ability to identify relationships, learn patterns, and make data-driven decisions, is fundamental to the development of autonomous AI. The foundation of autonomy is machine learning, which enables AI to process enormous volumes of data, develop itself, and function without continual human supervision. With an emphasis on various learning paradigms, self-learning systems, neural network designs, and the vital components of explainability and transparency, this chapter examines the basic machine learning concepts that support autonomous AI.

2.1 The Function of Reinforcement, Unsupervised, and Supervised Learning

Three primary categories can be used to broadly classify

machine learning:

- supervised learning, unsupervised learning, and reinforcement learning. Every one of these approaches contributes in a different way to giving autonomous AI the capacity to learn, adapt, and make wise choices.

Learning from Labeled Data: Supervised Learning

With supervised learning, AI learns from labeled datasets, that is, input data that has correspondingly accurate outputs using a task-driven approach. The model is perfect for tasks demanding high precision and structure since it is trained to identify correlations between inputs and outputs.

Autonomous AI supervised learning examples

- Computer vision for self-driving cars: AI models are trained to identify items such as traffic signals, pedestrians, and road signs.
- In order to identify future fraudulent activity, artificial intelligence (AI) examines previous fraudulent transactions.
- Speech recognition: Supervised learning is used by

virtual assistants such as Siri and Alexa to translate spoken words into text.

The drawbacks of supervised learning include the need for a significant amount of labeled data, which can be costly and time-consuming to acquire.
Generalization is difficult in dynamic settings where novel, unseen circumstances are common.

Unsupervised Education: Uncovering Hidden Trends

Unsupervised learning functions without labeled data, in contrast to supervised learning. The AI model finds structures, relationships, and patterns in unprocessed data. Because of this, it is very helpful for dimensionality reduction, grouping, and anomaly detection.

Autonomous AI examples of unsupervised learning

- Anomaly detection in cybersecurity: AI is able to identify possible cyberthreats by detecting anomalous network traffic patterns.
- Marketing customer segmentation: AI organizes clients according to their purchase history in order to

tailor recommendations.

- In a world without pre-made maps, artificial intelligence (AI) discovers spatial relationships.

Difficulties

- Difficulties with unsupervised learning: Since there are no established labels to direct the learning process, the findings may be challenging to interpret.
- Patterns that are statistically significant but not necessarily meaningful may be found by the AI.

Reinforcement Learning: Trial-and-error Decision Making

The most dynamic method is reinforcement learning (RL), which enables AI to learn by interacting with its surroundings and getting rewards or penalties according to its behavior. This kind of learning is essential for autonomous decision-making in real time.

Autonomous AI examples of reinforcement learning

- Self-driving cars: AI learns to drive by modifying steering, braking, and speed in response to rewards for safe travel.

- AI in robotics: Self-governing robots hone their motions to maximize efficiency in logistics and manufacturing.
- AI agents that play complex games, such as AlphaGo, are able to do so by constantly improving their strategy.

Difficulties with reinforcement learning

- Training takes a lot of time and processing resources.
- Inadequately constructed incentive schemes may result in unexpected AI actions.

These three strategies can be combined to help autonomous AI build advanced intelligence by utilizing structured learning (supervised), pattern discovery (unsupervised), and decision-making (reinforcement learning).

2.2 Continuous Learning and Self-Learning Systems

Conventional machine learning models need to be retrained whenever new data becomes available since they are dependent on static datasets. Autonomous AI must, however, function in dynamic settings with ever-changing circumstances. AI must be able to self-learn and continuously improve in order to accomplish this.

AI That Learns Without Overt Human Assistance: Self-Learning Systems

Self-education Without human direction, AI is able to expand its understanding and quickly adjust to new information. For AI systems functioning in real-world situations where pre-programmed instructions become obsolete, this is crucial.

Instances of self-learning AI

- Medical AI: AI is constantly updating its understanding of diseases based on patient data and fresh research.
- Autonomous cybersecurity systems: AI learns from previous attack patterns to adjust to changing cyberthreats.
- Personalized recommendation engines: As users interact with material, streaming services such as

Netflix and Spotify enhance their suggestions.

Ongoing Education: AI That Changes With Time

AI models can change without retraining thanks to continuous learning. AI gradually improves its settings rather than retraining from the beginning, guaranteeing that previous knowledge is kept while new information is integrated.

Key strategies in continuous learning

- Online learning: AI does not wait for batch processing; instead, it changes its models as new data comes in.
- Lifelong learning: AI learns from many tasks and applies that knowledge to new problems.
- Meta-learning: AI becomes adaptive across domains by learning how to learn.

Systems become more resilient, adaptive, and capable of long-term autonomy when self-learning and continuous learning are incorporated into AI models.

2.3 Autonomous Neural Network Architectures

The computational engines underlying autonomous AI are neural networks, which allow systems to process intricate inputs and reach their own conclusions. In autonomy, many structures have different functions.

Important Architectures for Neural Networks

- Convolutional neural networks, or CNNs, are made for pattern detection and image processing.
- Utilized in medical imaging AI, facial recognition, and self-driving cars.

AI can process speech, text, and time-series predictions by handling sequential data through the use of Recurrent Neural Networks (RNNs) and Long Short-Term Memory (LSTM) Networks.
Autonomous chatbots and language translation make use of it.

Transformers (e.g., GPT models)

- Facilitate the creation and comprehension of natural language.
- Real-time translation, content summary, and AI assistants are powerful features.

Generative Adversarial Networks (GANs)

- Produce artificial intelligence (AI) model training data.
- AI-driven simulations and picture enhancement make use of it.

When included into autonomous AI systems, these designs enable real-time perception, reasoning, and decision-making.

2.4 Transparency and Explainability in Autonomous AI Models

Assuring trustworthiness and accountability is one of the biggest obstacles in autonomous AI. Many AI models, especially deep learning systems, function as "black boxes," which means it is difficult to understand how they make decisions.

The Importance of Explainable AI (XAI)

Explainable AI (XAI) seeks to guarantee the ethical application of AI by:

- Give explained justifications for AI choices.
- Minimize unintended effects and bias.
- Facilitate human supervision and adherence to regulations.

Actions to Increase Transparency in AI

- Decision trees and linear regression are two examples of interpretable models that offer simple explanations.
- The examination of feature importance identifies the inputs that have an impact on AI choices.
- Visualization techniques: CNN heatmaps display the areas of images that AI is interested in.
- Rule-based explanations: AI programs produce written explanations for their results.

Keeping Performance and Explainability in Check

- Highly interpretable models are typically simpler but more trustworthy.
- Although deep learning models perform better, they need extra methods to be transparent.

Making sure autonomous AI systems' judgments are fair and explicable is crucial as they assume crucial roles in healthcare, finance, and security.

The foundation of autonomous AI is machine learning, which offers the intelligence, flexibility, and decision-making capabilities required for self-reliance. AI can reach previously unheard-of degrees of autonomy by applying supervised, unsupervised, and reinforcement learning, including self-learning and continuous learning, and employing advanced neural network architectures. However, confidence in AI is still very difficult to achieve without explainability and transparency.

CHAPTER 3

AUTONOMOUS AI SYSTEMS AND ROBOTICS

The limits of automation have been redrawn by the combination of robotics and artificial intelligence (AI), which allows robots to carry out increasingly complicated tasks with greater autonomy. AI-powered robotics is ushering in a new era of efficiency, accuracy, and adaptability in everything from industrial manufacturing to driverless cars and humanoid robots. This chapter examines the fundamental importance of artificial intelligence (AI) in robotics, the development of autonomous cars and drones, the revolution in industrial automation, and the potential applications of humanoid robots in the future.

3.1 AI's Incorporation into Robots

Conventional robotics performed repetitive operations using pre-programmed instructions. But because of artificial intelligence, robots can now learn, adapt, and make decisions in real time based on their surroundings. Robots can now operate in dynamic, unstructured contexts thanks to this integration, which has made the transition from strict, rule-based automation to intelligent autonomy possible.

Primary AI Robotics Technologies

Machine Learning and Deep Learning

AI-powered robots use machine learning algorithms to enhance their performance over time. They can recognize objects through supervised learning, recognize patterns through unsupervised learning, and improve their movements through trial and error through reinforcement learning.

Vision of Computers

Computer vision is used by robots with cameras and sensors to sense and comprehend their environment. They can travel and interact with people and items more easily thanks to sophisticated algorithms like object detection, facial recognition, and semantic segmentation.

Human speech can be processed and understood by AI-powered robots thanks to Natural Language Processing (NLP), which enables voice-controlled assistants, chatbots, and customer service robots. NLP enhances the user experience by facilitating smooth communication between people and machines.

Edge computing and cloud AI

Edge computing allows for low-latency decision-making by processing AI computations directly on the robot. By enabling robots to access large datasets and exchange information among a network of interconnected machines, cloud-based AI improves scalability.

Self-learning robots that can operate with little assistance from humans are now possible thanks to the combination of artificial intelligence and robotics, which has produced more autonomous, adaptive, and intelligent systems.

3.2 Self-Driving Cars and Drones

One of the biggest developments in AI-driven robotics is

the creation of self-driving cars and autonomous drones. By offering safer and more effective substitutes for human-operated machinery, these systems are revolutionizing transportation, surveillance, logistics, and emergency response.

Unmanned Aerial Vehicles

Unmanned aerial vehicles (UAVs), sometimes known as drones, have developed from remote-controlled gadgets to completely autonomous systems that can navigate on their own. To make judgments in real time, AI-powered drones use a combination of GPS, computer vision, sensor fusion, and reinforcement learning.

Autonomous Drone Applications

- Aerial Surveillance and Security: Drones with AI-powered cameras keep an eye on vast regions for disaster relief, wildlife preservation, and law enforcement.
- Agricultural Automation: Artificial intelligence (AI) drones assess crop health, identify insect infestations, and adjust irrigation schedules.

- Delivery Services: To cut down on transit times and expenses, companies such as UPS and Amazon are leading the way in drone-based delivery systems.
- Drones are used in disaster relief and emergency rescues by navigating dangerous environments during search and rescue operations.

Driverless Automobiles

Because they eliminate human error, reduce traffic congestion, and enhance road safety, self-driving cars and trucks are transforming the transportation sector. To navigate through challenging traffic situations, autonomous cars use AI models that analyze data from LiDAR, radar, GPS, and high-resolution cameras.

Important AI Technologies for Self-Driving Cars

In order to provide a thorough picture of the surroundings, Sensor Fusion integrates data from several sources, including LiDAR, cameras, and radar.

- The most effective routes are found by AI using Path Planning Algorithms; obstructions are avoided and speed is adjusted appropriately.

- Through simulated training, self-driving cars can enhance their driving skills thanks to deep reinforcement learning.

Difficulties and Ethical Issues

- Safety and Reliability: Autonomous systems need to be strong enough to manage unforeseen situations like pedestrian crossings and unexpected obstacles.
- Governments are still working on regulations to standardize and legalize self-driving technology.
- Liability Issues It is still difficult to determine who is responsible in accidents involving autonomous vehicles.

Notwithstanding these obstacles, developments in artificial intelligence are expanding the possibilities for complete autonomy in transportation, as autonomous trucks, delivery robots, and self-driving taxis become more and more feasible.

3.3 Industrial Automation with AI

Manufacturing has always relied heavily on industrial

automation, but artificial intelligence has greatly increased its potential. These days, factories are more productive and economical because to AI-driven robotic systems that are self-optimizing, predictive, and collaborative.

Industrial Robotics' Development

- The first industrial robots were designed to perform repetitive, predetermined tasks.
- Second-Generation Robots: With sensors, they could react to environmental changes.
- AI-powered robots with cognitive abilities, real-time decision-making, and predictive maintenance capabilities are known as Third-Generation Robots.

The use of artificial intelligence in industrial automation

Predictive Maintenance: AI examines historical records and sensor data to anticipate equipment breakdowns before they happen, reducing downtime.

- lowers maintenance expenses by not adhering to set schedules and simply replacing parts as needed.

Collaborative Robots (Cobots)

- Cobots work alongside humans, increasing productivity in assembly lines, quality control, and logistics, in contrast to typical robots that function independently.

- Cobots modify their actions in real time by utilizing adaptive AI and reinforcement learning.

Automated Quality Control

- AI-driven computer vision systems are more accurate than human inspectors in identifying flaws in production lines.

- Over time, machine learning models enhance fault detection, cutting waste and boosting productivity.

Supply Chain Optimization

- AI-powered logistics systems optimize delivery routing, demand forecasting, and inventory management.

- Robotic warehouses and autonomous forklifts increase productivity in retail fulfillment and e-commerce facilities.

By enabling people to concentrate on more complex activities while robots perform repetitive or hazardous jobs, artificial intelligence (AI) in industrial automation is not only improving productivity but also ensuring safety in hazardous situations.

3.4 Humanoid Robots' Future

Humanoid robots are the next frontier of robotics, as they are made to resemble humans in both look and behavior. Humanoid robots are designed for versatility and interaction with humans, whereas autonomous cars and industrial robots are tailored for particular jobs.

Humanoid Robotics Developments to Date

AI-Driven Motion and Dexterity:
- Humanoids can run, walk, and operate items with human-like accuracy thanks to reinforcement learning algorithms.
- Tesla's Optimus and Boston Dynamics' Atlas demonstrate sophisticated robotic dexterity and

locomotion.

Emotional AI and Human Interaction

- Humanoid robots such as Sophia and Ameca use natural language processing, voice synthesis, and face recognition to interact with people.
- These robots are able to identify and react to human emotions thanks to AI-driven emotional intelligence.

Humanoid Robots for Possible Uses

AI-powered humanoids help with physical therapy, medication reminders, and patient monitoring in the healthcare and elderly care sectors.

- Customer Service and Retail: In shopping centers, hotels, and airports, robots act as **interactive assistants**, answering questions.
- Space Exploration: In zero-gravity environments where human presence is restricted, humanoids could carry out exploration and maintenance duties.

Difficulties and Moral Issues

- The coexistence of humans and robots: striking a balance between automation and human employment issues.

- Ensuring that robots behave morally and in accordance with human ideals is known as AI Bias and Safety.

- Overcoming societal concerns over the integration of robots in daily life is the first step towards achieving public acceptance.

Humanoid robots will become more capable, autonomous, and emotionally aware as AI develops, changing how people interact with machines in both personal and professional settings.

A new era of autonomy, intelligence, and efficiency is being shaped by the combination of robots and artificial intelligence. AI-powered robotics is revolutionizing industries and redefining human-machine interaction, from self-learning industrial robots to self-driving cars and humanoid assistants. Even while there are still obstacles to overcome, continuous advancements in machine learning, sensor technology, and cognitive AI will drive robotics closer to complete autonomy and smooth social integration.

CHAPTER 4

Autonomous AI's Function in Finance and Business

Business and finance are not an exception to the way artificial intelligence is transforming industries at a rate never seen before. AI is helping businesses increase productivity, lower risks, and seize new growth prospects by automating financial decision-making and streamlining corporate procedures. The development of autonomous AI self-learning systems that function with little assistance from humans will have a major impact on how business strategy, entrepreneurship, and employment are shaped in the future.

This chapter examines how AI affects financial decision-making, how autonomous AI is changing the workforce, how corporate processes might be optimized, and how startups and entrepreneurial endeavors are affected.

4.1 AI in the Making of Financial Decisions

Although data-driven decision-making has long been a staple in the financial industry, AI has elevated it to new levels by offering real-time insights, predictive analytics, and automated trading capabilities. Financial institutions, hedge funds, and investment organizations are now driven by AI algorithms that make choices based on enormous volumes of real-time and historical data.

Financial Decision-Making: Key AI Applications

- Algorithmic Trading: AI-powered trading platforms examine market data, spot patterns, and place transactions when it's best to do so.
- High-frequency trading (HFT) allows businesses to profit from microsecond market inefficiencies by using artificial intelligence (AI) to process large datasets in milliseconds.
- Trading bots can improve their methods over time and adjust to changing market conditions thanks to deep reinforcement learning.

Fraud Detection and Risk Management

- AI models examine transaction patterns to instantly spot anomalies and possible fraud.

- By looking at alternative data sources, like social media activity and digital footprints, predictive analytics assists financial institutions in determining credit risk.

- Sensitive financial data is protected by AI-powered security systems that identify and eliminate online threats.

Personalized Financial Planning and Robo-Advisors

- AI-powered robo-advisors provide automated investment strategies, customizing portfolios according to customer financial objectives and risk tolerance.

- AI chatbots analyze spending patterns and offer budgetary advice, providing real-time financial guidance.

- By forecasting future financial situations based on economic data, predictive AI helps with retirement planning.

Financial institutions can improve decision-making speed, decrease human error, and develop individualized financial strategies by utilizing AI, which will benefit both businesses and investors.

4.2 The Self-Sustained AI Staff

AI systems are starting to fill positions that have historically been filled by human workers as they get more sophisticated. There are important concerns regarding the future of employment, productivity, and workplace dynamics raised by this move towards an autonomous AI workforce.

The Function of AI in Workforce Automation

Cognitive Process Automation (CPA)

- AI can learn, adapt, and make decisions independently thanks to CPA, in contrast to standard robotic process automation (RPA), which adheres to preset rules.
- AI can reduce the need for human labor by handling

legal document analysis, HR procedures, and consumer inquiries.

AI-Powered Decision Support Systems

- AI helps executives by offering data-driven recommendations, which improves operational effectiveness and strategic planning.
- Proactive decision-making is made possible by advanced AI models' ability to forecast market trends, consumer behavior, and supply chain disruptions.

AI as a Tool for Managers

- AI-powered analytics monitor worker performance and pinpoint areas in need of training and skill development.
- Workforce management is optimized by AI-powered scheduling solutions, which guarantee effective resource allocation and productivity.

Difficulties and Moral Issues

Job Displacement vs. Job Creation

- AI opens up new prospects in AI development, system monitoring, and ethics compliance, but it also replaces some monotonous tasks.
- In order to be relevant in AI-driven sectors, the workforce needs to reskill and adapt.

AI and Workplace Ethics

- AI-powered hiring algorithms must refrain from discrimination and bias during the hiring process.
- Privacy and autonomy issues are brought up by the use of AI for employee monitoring and productivity tracking.

Instead of completely replacing human workers, the autonomous AI workforce aims to augment human capabilities and free up workers to concentrate on higher-value jobs that call for critical thinking, creativity, and emotional intelligence.

4.3 Business Process Optimization Driven by AI

By streamlining workflows, improving decision-making, and automating procedures, AI is revolutionizing business operations. Companies that successfully use AI acquire a competitive edge through enhanced consumer experiences, lower costs, and increased efficiency.

AI in Supply Chain Management and Operations

Predictive Maintenance

- AI foresees equipment breakdowns before they happen, saving industrial and logistics companies money on downtime.
- Machine data is analyzed by IoT-enabled AI systems to find wear-and-tear trends.

Inventory and Demand Forecasting.

- AI algorithms analyze market trends, past sales data, and outside variables to optimize inventory levels through Inventory and Demand Forecasting.
- AI-driven robotic fulfillment systems are used in automated warehouses to improve the accuracy and speed of logistics.

AI in Procurement and Supplier Management

- AI-driven systems for procurement **determine

prospects for cost savings and maximize supplier bargaining.

- AI improves fraud detection and contract management, guaranteeing adherence to legal requirements.

AI in Customer Experience and Marketing

AI-powered chatbots and virtual assistants 24/7

- AI-powered customer support bots answer questions around-the-clock, cutting down on wait times and increasing user happiness.
- AI may determine client emotions through sentiment analysis, enabling tailored answers.

Dynamic Pricing and Personalization

- AI uses market demand, competition pricing, and consumer behavior to instantly modify product prices.
- Conversion rates are increased by hyper-personalized ads and recommendations generated by machine learning models.

Businesses may achieve more agility, optimize resources, and drive innovation by incorporating AI into their operations, which will result in long-term, steady development.

4.4 AI in Startups and Entrepreneurship

AI is democratizing technology access and empowering entrepreneurs to create data-driven, scalable enterprises. Businesses can obtain a competitive edge in congested markets by using AI to automate procedures, analyze customer information, and optimize product development.

The Effect of AI on Startup Development

- AI tools scrape data from several sources to identify industry trends, consumer wants, and rival strategies. This is known as AI-Driven Market Research and Competitive Analysis.
- Natural language processing, or NLP, gathers information from online reviews, patents, and news stories.

- Time-to-market is decreased by rapid prototyping and product testing aided by AI-powered design tools and automated product development and prototyping.
- Generative AI is useful for developing branding strategies, UI/UX design, and marketing content.

Smart Funding and Investment Decision-Making

- AI-driven systems use business profiles to pair startups with the right investors and funding opportunities.
- AI helps entrepreneurs improve their pitches by analyzing funding trends and investor opinion.

Difficulties for Startups Using AI

- It is imperative for startups to make sure AI systems comply with data protection laws like the CCPA and GDPR.
- Transparent algorithms and bias mitigation strategies are necessary for the development of ethical AI.

Personnel Acquisition and Technical Expertise

- AI-driven startups are in need of specialized personnel since they require individuals with expertise in machine learning, data science, and AI ethics.
- The talent gap can be closed by collaborations with AI research institutions and tech firms.

Notwithstanding these obstacles, AI is promoting innovation, reducing barriers to entry for new businesses, and creating entrepreneurial opportunities in numerous industries.

Because autonomous AI improves decision-making, optimizes processes, and reshapes labor dynamics, it is revolutionizing business and finance. AI is generating more efficient, intelligent, and scalable businesses, from startup ideas and process automation to AI-powered trading platforms and autonomous workforce management. The advantages of AI-driven change greatly exceed the drawbacks, even while ethical issues and labor disruptions need to be addressed. Businesses that strategically use AI will be at the forefront of economic growth and digital innovation in the future.

CHAPTER 5

Autonomous AI and Healthcare

Artificial intelligence's introduction into the medical field has transformed patient care, diagnosis, and therapy. AI-driven solutions are improving early disease diagnosis, automating repetitive procedures, and improving the accuracy of medical judgments. The rise of autonomous AI in healthcare is changing the dynamic between patients, doctors, and technology, not just increasing productivity.

The evolution of robotic surgery and autonomous healthcare assistants, predictive healthcare and epidemiology, the ethical issues surrounding AI-driven medical applications, and the role of AI in medical diagnoses and treatment are all covered in this chapter.

5.1 AI in Medical Treatment and Diagnosis

Accuracy and early detection are critical components of

medical diagnostics. To diagnose illnesses, doctors typically use lab testing, patient history, and expertise. However, new levels of speed and accuracy have been brought about by AI-driven diagnostic tools, which have decreased human error and allowed for early intervention.

AI in Imaging and Disease Detection

One of the most notable fields where AI has had an impact is medical imaging. High-precision X-ray, MRI, CT, and ultrasound analysis is possible with AI-powered devices.

- Deep learning systems are able to identify abnormalities in medical scans more quickly than human radiologists.
- AI improves the early diagnosis of diseases such organ anomalies, fractures, and cancers.
- AI increases diagnostic confidence by lowering false positives and negatives.

AI helps with biopsy sample analysis and more accurate malignant cell detection in pathology and cancer detection.

- On the basis of past patient data, machine learning

models forecast the course of a disease.

ECG Analysis Driven by AI and Cardiology

- AI detects abnormal cardiac rhythms and forecasts problems like atrial fibrillation.
- AI-powered real-time ECG monitoring improves cardiovascular disease early diagnosis.

AI in Tailored Therapy Programs

By customizing medical care to meet the needs of each patient, AI is revolutionizing treatment approaches.

Precision Medicine

- AI uses genetic data to identify the best medications and treatments for individual patients.
- By predicting how people would react to drugs, machine learning models help prevent negative drug responses.

AI-Assisted medication Discovery

- AI predicts the efficacy of drugs and analyzes molecular structures to speed up medication development.

- AI finds possible compounds more quickly, which cuts down on the amount of time needed for clinical studies.

Healthcare practitioners can create individualized treatment plans that enhance patient outcomes and provide quicker, more accurate diagnoses by utilizing AI.

5.2 Autonomous Healthcare Assistants and Robotic Surgery

Artificial intelligence (AI)-driven robotic devices are improving surgical results while reducing human limits since surgical operations demand extraordinary precision.

AI-Driven Precision and Robotic Surgery

Robotic technologies driven by AI let surgeons carry out intricate treatments more precisely.

- Robotic arms with AI assistance create smaller incisions during minimally invasive surgery, which shortens recovery times and minimizes problems.

- During procedures, surgeons can see more clearly thanks to real-time AI analysis.

AI-Guided Decision Support

- AI evaluates surgical data to recommend the best methods and strategies.
- AI lowers the margin of error in robotic-assisted surgeries by improving hand-eye coordination.

Remote and Autonomous Surgery

- AI makes it possible for elite doctors to perform robotic surgery remotely, operating on patients in far-off places.
- Fully autonomous robotic surgeries, in which artificial intelligence (AI) devices carry out operations without direct human involvement, are still being researched.

Self-sufficient Medical Assistants

AI-powered robotic aides are revolutionizing hospital administration and patient care beyond surgery.

- Artificial Intelligence-Powered Nursing Assistants
- AI-powered robots help with mobility, give medication, and keep an eye on patients.
- Reminders for post-operative care and medication adherence are given by smart assistants.

AI in Rehabilitation and Elderly Care

- Paralyzed individuals can relearn movement with the aid of robotic exoskeletons.
- AI-powered virtual therapists support cognitive rehabilitation and mental wellbeing.

Healthcare systems can increase accuracy, lower medical errors, and improve patient experiences by incorporating AI into surgical processes and patient care.

5.3 AI-Driven Epidemiology and Predictive Healthcare

Predictive and preventive medicine is replacing reactive healthcare thanks to AI. AI is capable of predicting disease outbreaks, identifying personal health concerns, and allocating healthcare resources as efficiently as possible by evaluating enormous volumes of patient data.

Predictive Healthcare using AI

Early Disease Detection

- AI algorithms identify possible health hazards by analyzing genetics, lifestyle choices, and medical history.
- Real-time data collection by wearable medical devices warns physicians and patients of potential problems.

Management of Chronic Diseases

- AI-driven systems monitor diabetes, high blood pressure, and other long-term illnesses, assisting patients in better health management.
- AI makes lifestyle suggestions to stop the course of disease.

AI in Forecasting Mental Health

- AI looks for indications of anxiety or depression by analyzing social media activity, speech patterns, and facial expressions.

- AI-driven chatbots offer therapeutic advice and mental health help.

AI in Public Health and Epidemiology

AI is essential for monitoring and controlling disease outbreaks on a worldwide basis.

Pandemic Prediction and Response

- AI algorithms forecast the spread of disease by analyzing global travel trends, climatic data, and infection rates.
- AI helps governments create targeted vaccination campaigns and lockdown plans.

AI in Vaccine Development

- By recognizing viral components and forecasting immune responses, AI speeds up vaccine research.
- AI-powered models evaluate the effectiveness of vaccines prior to clinical trials.

Public Health Monitoring

- AI identifies at-risk groups by examining social

determinants of health and hospital admission data.

- Chatbots driven by AI inform communities on ways to prevent illness and available treatments.

Medical practitioners can avert health emergencies, efficiently distribute resources, and enhance public health outcomes by utilizing AI for epidemiology and predictive healthcare.

5.4 Ethical Issues in Healthcare Driven by AI

Even if AI significantly improves healthcare, there are still moral and legal issues that need to be resolved.

Data Security and Privacy

Patient Data Protection

- AI systems need enormous volumes of patient data, which raises questions regarding data misuse and breaches. Ensuring patient confidentiality requires strict adherence to laws like GDPR and HIPAA.

Bias in AI Decision-Making

- AI algorithms may be biased based on training data, which could result in different recommendations for diagnosis and treatment.
- To eradicate socioeconomic, racial, and gender biases, transparent AI development is required.

Medical Liability and Accountability

Legal Implications of AI-Driven Diagnoses

- Determining culpability in the event that an AI system diagnoses a patient incorrectly is still a challenging task.
- To establish accountability amongst hospitals, medical experts, and AI developers, clear criteria are required.

Autonomy vs. Human Oversight

- AI should be used in conjunction with human medical knowledge, not in substitute of it.
- In situations where life is at stake, doctors must continue to have the last say in decisions.

Ethical Application of AI in Care for the Dying

AI in Palliative Care

- AI models help with end-of-life planning and forecast patient decline.
- The use of AI in making decisions on life-extending therapies raises ethical questions.

Moral Dilemmas in AI-Driven Mental Health Care

- AI chatbots offer treatment, but they are not as emotionally intelligent or empathetic as humans.
- Care gaps could result from an over-reliance on AI for mental health therapy.

Ethical frameworks must be created to strike a balance between innovation and patient rights, safety, and equity as AI continues to revolutionize healthcare.

By enhancing public health management, predictive medicine, surgical accuracy, and diagnostics, artificial intelligence is changing the healthcare industry. Nonetheless, there are advantages and disadvantages to the development of autonomous AI in healthcare. Although AI improves medical accessibility, accuracy, and efficiency, ethical issues pertaining to data privacy, bias, and liability need to be properly addressed. By incorporating AI properly, healthcare workers may utilize its full potential to change medical care, enhance patient outcomes, and build a more efficient and equitable healthcare system.

CHAPTER 6

SELF-GOVERNING AI IN DEFENSE AND SECURITY

The way threats are identified, stopped, and defeated has changed as a result of the use of artificial intelligence into security and combat. AI has become an essential tool in cybersecurity, surveillance, fraud detection, and military operations due to its capacity to scan enormous volumes of data, spot trends, and react to threats instantly. However, there are benefits and moral conundrums associated with the development of autonomous AI in many domains.

This chapter examines the capabilities, hazards, and difficulties of striking a balance between security and moral responsibility as they relate to artificial intelligence (AI) in cybersecurity, surveillance, financial security, and military warfare.

6.1 AI in Threat Detection and Cybersecurity

The increasing sophistication of cybersecurity threats necessitates the use of proactive and clever defenses. Antivirus software and firewalls are examples of traditional security measures that are no longer adequate to stop sophisticated cyberattacks. Security solutions driven by AI have become a powerful tool for spotting and eliminating threats before they do any harm.

The Function of AI in Threat Identification

Cybersecurity systems powered by AI examine network traffic, spot irregularities, and react instantly to online threats.

- Artificial Intelligence (AI) keeps an eye on network activity and spots odd trends that might point to a cyberattack.
- Before ransomware, phishing attempts, and malware infiltrate systems, machine learning models identify them.

Anomaly Detection and Behavioral Analysis

- Unusual data transfers or illegal access are examples

of departures from typical user behavior that AI can detect.

- Self-learning algorithms get better over time and adjust to new threats.

Automated Incident Response

- AI-driven security systems are able to neutralize cyberthreats on their own without assistance from humans.

- Because AI speeds up reaction times, cyberattacks have less of an impact.

Predictive cybersecurity using AI

To predict possible security breaches, predictive AI models examine data from previous cyberattacks.

Threat Intelligence and Risk Assessment

- AI identifies new cybersecurity threats by correlating data from various sources.

- Organizations can improve security before an attack happens by using predictive models.

AI-Powered Deception Technology

- AI creates fictitious data and systems to trick hackers.
- Automated honeypots entice intruders and collect information about their strategies.

Cybercriminals are using AI to launch increasingly sophisticated attacks, despite the fact that AI improves cybersecurity. This has resulted in a continuous arms race between malicious actors and security experts.

6.2 Privacy Issues with AI-Powered Surveillance

Artificial intelligence (AI)-driven technologies that can track people, analyze their behavior, and identify suspicious activity in real time have replaced manual monitoring in surveillance systems. AI-powered surveillance is used by governments and organizations to improve security, but it has also given rise to grave worries about civil liberties and privacy.

AI in Facial Recognition and Video Surveillance

Large volumes of visual data are processed accurately by AI-enhanced surveillance systems.

Facial Recognition Technology

- AI uses facial features to identify people, allowing for automated security monitoring and access control.
- AI is used by law enforcement to find missing people and criminals.

AI is capable of identifying anomalous crowd behavior, including possible riots or panic episodes.

- Predictive AI aids in averting security breaches and societal unrest.

License Plate Recognition (LPR)

- AI reads and compares license plates to databases for traffic monitoring and law enforcement.
- AI-powered parking enforcement and toll collecting systems increase productivity.

The Ethical Argument: Privacy vs. Security

- AI-powered surveillance improves security, but it also jeopardizes personal liberties.

Mass Surveillance and Government Control

- AI-powered monitoring systems can be utilized for political control and suppression of opposition.
- Countries with authoritarian regimes deploy AI for social grading and citizen surveillance.

Data Collection and Privacy Violations

- AI surveillance systems capture enormous volumes of personal data, prompting concerns about data misuse.
- Lack of clear regulations can lead to unauthorized data sharing and breaches.

Bias and Discrimination in AI Surveillance

- AI facial recognition algorithms have shown racial and gender biases, leading to wrongful identifications.
- Ethical AI development is necessary to prevent discrimination and misuse.

While AI-powered surveillance improves public safety, it must be implemented with strict ethical guidelines and oversight to prevent abuses.

6.3 AI in Fraud Detection and Financial Security

Financial fraud is a growing global threat, with hackers utilizing new ways to exploit vulnerabilities in banking and financial systems. AI-powered fraud detection systems have become vital in spotting questionable transactions, averting financial losses, and protecting customers.

Using AI to Identify Fraud

By examining trends and identifying irregularities in financial transactions, artificial intelligence improves fraud detection.

Anomaly Detection and Transaction Monitoring

- AI monitors expenditure trends and identifies variations that might point to fraud.
- Financial institutions are alerted to questionable activity in real time.

Credit Card Fraud Prevention

- AI analyzes device information, location data, and purchase patterns to identify fraudulent transactions.
- Machine learning algorithms reduce false positives while improving fraud detection accuracy.

Identity Theft and Account Takeover Prevention

- AI-powered biometric authentication ensures secure user identification.
- AI detects unusual login behavior and stops unwanted access.

AI in Financial Security and Risk Management

AI enhances decision-making and risk assessment, which increases financial security.

AI in Anti-Money Laundering (AML)

- AI recognizes money laundering techniques including layering and structured transactions.
- Financial organizations can comply with regulations with the aid of automated compliance solutions.

AI in the Detection of Insurance Fraud

- AI examines insurance claims to identify fraudulent behavior.
- AI-powered forensic analysis helps discover phony accident reports and false medical claims.

AI in Stock Market Security

- AI monitors stock trading actions for evidence of market manipulation.
- AI-driven predictive analytics help investors spot dangers and avoid fraudulent schemes.

Financial security is strengthened by AI-powered fraud detection, but thieves are always coming up with new ways to avoid detection, thus AI must constantly advance.

6.4 Autonomous AI's Ascent in Combat

With the introduction of autonomous weaponry, battlefield analytics, and AI-driven strategy creation, the incorporation of AI into military operations has revolutionized contemporary warfare. AI increases military effectiveness, but it also brings up moral and geopolitical issues.

Autonomous Weapons Driven by AI

AI-powered weapons are more effective in combat because they require less human involvement.

Unmanned Aerial Vehicles (UAVs) and Drones

- AI-controlled drones carry out targeted attacks, reconnaissance, and surveillance.
- Swarms of autonomous drones cooperate to conduct coordinated military actions.

AI in Missile Defense and Guidance Systems

- AI improves combat accuracy by enhancing precision-guided missile targeting.
- Defense systems powered by AI identify and eliminate incoming threats.

Robotic Combat Units on the Ground

- Robotic soldiers with AI capabilities carry out combat and reconnaissance tasks.

- Autonomous vehicles and tanks lessen the number of people killed in combat.

AI in Battlefield Analytics and Military Strategy

AI uses real-time data analysis to improve military operations decision-making.

Battlefield Surveillance Driven by AI

- AI analyzes drone and satellite photos to find adversary movements.
- AI optimizes force deployment and forecasts conflict situations.

Cyber Warfare and AI-Driven Hacking

- AI strengthens military networks' cybersecurity defenses.
- Cyberattacks driven by AI interfere with hostile infrastructure and communications.

AI in Strategy Planning and War Simulations

- AI models assist military strategists improve their strategies by simulating combat situations.

- AI supports mission planning, resource allocation, and logistics.

Ethical and Legal Difficulties with AI in Combat

Warfare powered by AI raises serious moral and legal issues.

Accountability for AI-Powered Attacks

- It is still difficult to establish who is legally responsible for military operations powered by AI.
- To avoid unexpected casualties, ethical AI development is essential.

Autonomous AI and the Risk of Uncontrolled Warfare:

Without human supervision, AI-powered weapons have the potential to intensify conflicts.

- To stop AI-driven arms races, regulations are required.

AI and the Danger of International Cyber-warfare

- Cyberattacks driven by AI have the potential to seriously harm national security infrastructures.

- The establishment of cybersecurity treaties requires international cooperation.

To avoid unforeseen repercussions, the growing use of AI in combat necessitates a careful balancing act between ethical issues and technological breakthroughs.

By improving threat identification, fraud prevention, surveillance, and military operations, artificial intelligence (AI) has completely changed security and combat. Although AI-powered security solutions increase security, they also bring up moral questions about accountability, privacy, and human rights. AI has strategic benefits in military applications, but there is a serious risk of conflict escalation on its own. To guarantee that AI is applied morally in security and combat, responsible AI development and international rules are crucial.

CHAPTER 7

Autonomous AI's Risks and Difficulties

Artificial intelligence (AI) systems pose a number of risks and challenges that need to be properly managed as they become more autonomous. Although AI can transform industries, improve decision-making, and boost productivity, its independence also raises serious issues with bias, security flaws, ambiguities in the law, moral quandaries, and existential threats.

This chapter examines the main risks and challenges of autonomous AI, including the contentious fear of AI singularity, security threats, ethical and legal ramifications, and bias and fairness issues.

7.1 The Fairness and Bias Issue in AI

Artificial intelligence (AI) systems are frequently praised for their capacity to process enormous volumes of data and reach unbiased conclusions. They are not, however, intrinsically impartial. When AI algorithms are trained on historical data, they will unavoidably inherit and magnify any biases present in the data.

Comprehending AI Prejudice

When algorithms generate consistently biased results as a result of faulty data, poor design decisions, or unexpected outcomes from machine learning models, this is known as AI bias. Bias can appear in many forms, such as:

- Historical Bias: AI that has been trained on historical data that reflects societal biases will keep reinforcing them. For instance, if hiring practices historically favored men, hiring algorithms trained on decades of employment data might favor male candidates.
- Sampling Bias: The AI model may give preference to some groups over others if the training data does not fairly reflect the diversity of the real world. For example, biased training data has been found to make facial recognition technology less accurate in identifying people with darker skin tones.

- Algorithmic Bias: Some biases stem from the design of the AI model itself. Certain machine learning techniques may unintentionally weigh certain features more heavily, leading to unfair outcomes.

Real-World Consequences of AI Bias

- Discriminatory Hiring Practices: AI-driven recruitment tools have been found to favor certain demographic groups over others, leading to unfair hiring decisions.
- Racial and Gender Bias in Law Enforcement AI: Predictive policing AI has disproportionately targeted minority communities, reinforcing systemic discrimination.
- Inequitable Healthcare AI Models: AI models in healthcare have occasionally underdiagnosed diseases in marginalized populations due to skewed training data.

Addressing AI Bias and Ensuring Fairness

Mitigating AI bias requires a multi-faceted approach:

- Diverse and Representative Data: Ensuring AI models are trained on balanced and inclusive datasets.
- Bias Auditing and Transparency: Conducting regular audits of AI systems to detect and correct biases.
- Ethical AI Development: Incorporating fairness restrictions in AI models and creating accountability among AI developers.

AI bias remains a key impediment to fairness and equity, needing continuing monitoring, regulatory oversight, and continuous advancements in AI design.

7.2 Security Risks of Fully Autonomous AI

The rising autonomy of AI systems creates severe security risks. As AI becomes more capable of making judgments without human interaction, the potential for cyber attacks, manipulation, and system breakdowns increases.

AI-Powered Cyber Threats

- Autonomous Hacking: AI can be used both defensively and offensively in cybersecurity. Malicious actors can employ AI to construct self-learning malware that adapts to security safeguards.

- Data Poisoning Attacks: Attackers can control AI models by giving them deceptive data, prompting them to make wrong conclusions.

- Adversarial AI Attacks: Cybercriminals can abuse AI models by quietly modifying inputs, leading to inaccurate classifications or actions. AI-powered security cameras, for instance, may misidentify a threat if a picture is slightly altered.

Autonomous AI's Physical Security Risks

- Autonomous Weapons and Drones: AI-powered weapons are susceptible to hacking, hijacking, and misuse, which can have unexpected military repercussions.

- Self-Driving Vehicles and Transportation Risks:AI-powered self-driving cars may be vulnerable to hacking, which could result in disastrous malfunctions.

- Critical Infrastructure Vulnerabilities: AI is being employed in managing power grids, water supplies, and transportation networks. Such technologies could have catastrophic societal repercussions from a security compromise.

Methods to Reduce the Risks of AI Security

- Sturdy AI Security Frameworks: Creating cybersecurity guidelines specifically for AI.
- Explainable AI and Transparency: Making sure AI choices are auditable and comprehensible in order to avoid security flaws.
- Regulatory Oversight: To avoid abuse, governments and organizations need to work together on AI security regulations.

Security concerns will only increase as AI systems become more prevalent and powerful, thus proactive steps to protect AI technologies are required.

7.3 AI Autonomy's Ethical and Legal Challenges

Society has not yet fully addressed the complicated ethical and legal issues raised by the development of autonomous AI.

AI Autonomy's Legal Difficulties

- Accountability and Liability: It is difficult to assign blame when an autonomous AI system causes harm. For instance, who should be held accountable in the event of a collision involving a self-driving car: the owner, the software developer, or the manufacturer?

- Control of AI in High-Risk Industries: AI is being incorporated into law enforcement, healthcare, banking, and military applications. Governments find it difficult to control its use while striking a balance between public safety and innovation.

- Created Work by AI and Intellectual Property Rights: AI-generated content presents ownership and copyright concerns. Who owns the rights if an AI system creates a new technology, writes a novel, or composes music?

AI Autonomy's Ethical Issues

- AI-Powered Moral Decision-Making: There may be moral conundrums for autonomous AI systems in which there is no obvious right or wrong response. For example, a self-driving automobile might have to choose between swerving into another car or colliding with a person.

- Decrease in Human Supervision: Human decision-making becomes less important as AI systems get more autonomous, which raises questions about uncritical faith in AI.

- AI Taking Over Human Jobs: AI increases productivity, but automation also poses a danger to millions of jobs, sparking ethical discussions about economic displacement.

Governments, legal professionals, and ethicists must collaborate to develop frameworks that guarantee AI autonomy does not result in immoral or illegal outcomes in order to address these issues.

7.4 The Fear of AI Singularity

The term "AI singularity" describes the speculative moment when AI surpasses human intelligence and loses control. Philosophers, technologists, and scientists have all argued about this idea extensively.

Comprehending the Singularity of AI

The premise behind the fear of singularity is that when AI surpasses humans in intelligence, it may:

- Self-Improve Exponentially: AI has the potential to recursively increase its own intelligence, surpassing human capacity at a rapid pace.
- In the absence of human-aligned objectives, a sophisticated AI may act in ways that are detrimental to or unconcerned about people.
- An artificial intelligence (AI) that has unfettered access to financial systems, military hardware, and global infrastructure could pose a serious existential danger.

Is the Singularity of AI a Realistic Fear?

Even though AI has advanced significantly, general intelligence is still a long way off. But other specialists have different views:

- Optimists think AI will continue to be a tool under human control as long as appropriate safeguards are in place to avoid singularity.
- AI singularity, according to skeptics, is a far-fetched, hypothetical idea without any hard data to back it up.
- Even though singularity is unlikely, AI development should still be carefully managed to prevent unforeseen consequences, according to Cautionary Experts.

Avoidance of Unchecked AI Development

Alignment with Human Values

- Making sure AI systems give ethical and human-centered objectives first priority.
- AI Safety study: Conducting rigorous study on AI

control systems and fail-safes.

- International AI Governance: Establishing worldwide policies to regulate AI development and avoid uncontrolled AI expansion.

Autonomous AI brings great opportunities but also serious concerns that must be carefully managed. Bias and fairness challenges test AI's impartiality, security dangers jeopardize vital systems, legal and ethical ambiguities generate regulatory difficulties, and the dread of AI singularity fuels existential concerns. To fully harness AI's potential while reducing its risks, interdisciplinary collaboration among AI researchers, politicians, security experts, and ethicists is crucial.

CHAPTER 8

Autonomous AI's Effect on Society

Artificial intelligence's (AI) growing independence is changing many facets of human existence, including social interactions, public trust, work, and education. As AI develops further, its impact becomes more widespread in society, influencing public views, learning systems, economies, and cultural norms in addition to technological applications.

With an emphasis on the future of labor, AI's role in education, its impact on social interactions, and the degree of trust society has in AI systems, this chapter examines the complex implications of autonomous AI. We may gain a better understanding of the advantages and difficulties associated with AI-driven change by closely exploring these areas.

8.1 AI-Driven Unemployment and the Future of Work

The effect that autonomous AI would have on jobs is among the biggest worries. The global workforce is undergoing a time of unparalleled change as AI systems gain the ability to execute activities that were previously only possible by humans.

Automation and Employment Losses

Human work is already being replaced by AI-driven automation in a number of areas, especially in:

- The demand for human labor in industries has decreased as automated robots have replaced monotonous and dangerous jobs in manufacturing and production.
- The need for human support agents is declining as AI-powered chatbots and virtual assistants handle more and more client inquiries in call centers and customer service.
- Logistics and Transportation: Drones, robotic warehouse workers, and autonomous cars are

changing supply chain operations by reducing the need for human drivers and logistics staff.

- Financial Services: AI-powered algorithms can currently outperform human analysts in stock trading, risk analysis, and fraud detection.

The Increase in Demand for Reskilling and New Jobs

Automation powered by AI may replace some occupations, but it also opens up new opportunities:

- AI Development and Maintenance: Machine learning experts, data scientists, and AI engineers will be in more demand as AI use rises.
- The roles of human-AI collaboration Professionals will be needed in many businesses to collaborate with AI, deciphering its findings and formulating strategic plans.
- Governance of AI Ethics: To ensure responsible deployment, the emergence of AI calls for experts in ethics, compliance, and governance.

Workforce Adaptation and Policy Reactions

Governments, corporations, and educational institutions need to do the following to reduce AI-driven unemployment:

- The promotion of reskilling programs aims to provide displaced workers with AI-related skills by funding workforce retraining.
- Promoting lifelong learning by developing flexible educational models that assist employees in constantly improving their skill sets.
- Implementing Universal Basic Income (UBI) Discussions: Examining economic strategies that help people in a future when artificial intelligence (AI) performs an increasing amount of labor.

AI is redefining employment, not just destroying them. Making sure that employees can successfully move into new roles that enhance AI rather than compete with it is the difficult part.

8.2 AI in Lifelong Learning and Education

AI has the power to completely transform education by increasing accessibility, efficiency, and personalization of learning. Autonomous AI is revolutionizing the way people learn, from intelligent tutoring systems to AI-powered course recommendations.

Adaptive AI Tutors and Personalized Learning

The potential of AI in education to customize learning experiences to meet the needs of each individual is among its most exciting features. Platforms with AI capabilities can:

- Analyze Student Performance: AI systems are able to monitor a student's development and modify instructional materials as necessary.
- Offer Real-Time Feedback: AI instructors may provide prompt corrections and recommendations, which speeds up the learning process.
- In contrast to conventional educational approaches, AI is able to provide personalized study schedules depending on a student's skills and limitations.

Filling up the Gaps in Education

Additionally, AI is reducing educational inequalities by:

- AI-powered learning platforms enable students from underserved and remote places to receive top-notch instruction, hence expanding access to education.
- Aiding with Special Education Needs AI-powered solutions that provide text-to-speech, speech recognition, and individualized learning approaches can help kids with impairments.
- Enabling Lifelong Learning AI makes it easier for professionals to continue their education by providing them with flexible, on-demand learning programs.

Difficulties and Ethical Issues in AI-Powered Education

Even though AI improves education, there are still issues:

- AI-powered learning platforms gather enormous volumes of student data, which raises concerns about security and privacy.

- Algorithmic Bias: AI training data that lacks diversity may actually exacerbate rather than lessen educational disparities.

- Decreased Human Interaction: An over-reliance on AI in education may result in the loss of important human components like social learning and mentoring.

AI is changing education, but its benefits must be distributed fairly to all students, thus its implementation must be done carefully.

8.3 Artificial Intelligence and the Changing Social Environment

AI is changing how people connect, communicate, and build relationships in areas other than job and education. Artificial intelligence (AI)-driven technologies have a profound and subtle impact on social norms and human behavior as they become more integrated into daily life.

AI in Communication and Social Interactions

AI-driven communication technologies have changed how people connect with one another:

- AI Chatbots and Virtual Companions: With AI-powered chatbots now able to have meaningful conversations, concerns around emotional dependence on AI companions are being raised.
- A large portion of what users view on social media sites is determined by artificial intelligence (AI), which also shapes public conversation and reinforces preconceptions.
- The distinction between artificially generated and actual material is becoming increasingly hazy due to AI-generated content, which includes deepfake videos and articles.

AI's Ethical Consequences for Society

There are ethical issues regarding AI's impact on social norms:

- A reduction in in-person contacts and emotional

depth in relationships may result from excessive AI-mediated communication.

- Manipulation and Misinformation: Deepfake material and AI-powered propaganda can be used to disseminate false information and influence public opinion.
- Concerns regarding the degradation of civil liberties and privacy are raised by AI-powered facial recognition and data tracking.

To make sure AI strengthens real human interactions rather than undermines them, society must carefully manage these changes.

8.4 Perception and Trust of AI Systems by the Public

Public trust is essential for AI to be widely used. Even if AI has many benefits, people's adoption of it will rely on how they view its safety, fairness, and dependability.

Aspects Affecting Public Confidence in AI

The following factors influence public trust in AI:

- Transparency and Explainability: To win over users, AI judgments need to be comprehensible and justified.
- Bias and Fairness Issues: Discriminatory AI cases erode confidence and breed public mistrust.
- AI Failures and Safety Concerns: Mistakes involving AI systems, such crashes involving self-driving cars, can erode trust and impede the adoption of AI.

Establishing Public Trust in AI

In order to promote confidence in AI systems, stakeholders need to:

- Improve AI Transparency: Developers should improve the interpretability of AI decision-making processes.
- The development and application of AI should be guided by well-defined ethical frameworks.
- Involve the Public in AI Policy Discussions: Inclusive discussions about AI regulation and its effects on society can guarantee that AI is in line

with public ideals.

It takes careful planning, openness, and constant ethical concerns to gain people's trust in AI.

Autonomous AI is changing society by impacting social interactions, public trust, education, and jobs. AI-driven automation offers solutions that improve learning, communication, and efficiency, but it also poses problems like employment displacement and moral conundrums. Proactive governance, moral development, and making sure AI works in humanity's best interests are the keys to controlling its effects. A balanced strategy is required as AI develops further in order to optimize its advantages while reducing its risks.

CHAPTER 9

AUTONOMOUS AI's FUTURE

Artificial intelligence's (AI) quick development has already changed human interactions, economies, and businesses. The AI revolution is far from over, though. In the upcoming decades, artificial intelligence (AI) is expected to play an even more revolutionary role as researchers continue to push the limits of machine learning, deep learning, and neural networks.

This chapter examines important areas of advancement and innovation as it relates to the future trajectory of autonomous AI. It explores the development of artificial general intelligence (AGI), its application to space travel and colonization, the prospects for smart cities, and an outlook on how AI will change over the next fifty years.

9.1 The Road to Artificial General Intelligence (AGI)

Artificial General Intelligence (AGI): A Definition

Artificial General Intelligence (AGI) is the term used to describe AI that can execute any intellectual task that a human can because it has cognitive capacities similar to those of a human. In contrast to narrow AI, which is intended for specialized tasks like natural language processing or facial recognition, AGI would:

- AGI would not just be dependent on pre-programmed information; it would also be able to learn, reason, and adjust to new situations on its own.

- AGI would be able to think creatively, abstractly, and make decisions that are not only based on preset algorithms if it possessed reasoning and problem-solving abilities.

- Exhibit common sense: Artificial General Intelligence (AGI) would comprehend and react to real-world circumstances in a nuanced way, in contrast to current AI, which has trouble with context and ambiguity.

Main Obstacles in the Development of AGI

The road to AGI is still unclear despite tremendous advancements in AI because of several barriers:

- Current artificial intelligence models are data-driven pattern recognizers with a lack of actual understanding of concepts and meaning.
- AGI would necessitate enormous quantities of energy and processing capacity, which would raise questions around resource distribution and sustainability.
- Ethical and Safety Risks: A fully autonomous AGI may behave in an unpredictable manner, making it challenging to regulate or conform to human ideals.

AGI Development Steps

AGI is being actively pursued by researchers and tech firms by:

- AI is getting closer to AGI capabilities thanks to developments in deep learning architectures like transformer models and reinforcement learning.

- AGI must be able to apply knowledge from one area to another without requiring extensive retraining in order to improve its ability to transfer learning.

- Integrating AI with Neuroscience: To construct more flexible and adaptive AI systems, some methods for developing AGI entail simulating the neurological processes of the human brain.

Although it will probably take decades to reach AGI, as AI models advance, it may not be a question of if but when AGI will appear.

9.2 AI in Colonization and Space Exploration

The Contribution of AI to the Progress of Space Exploration

By enabling autonomous decision-making in deep space, boosting robotic missions, and improving data processing, artificial intelligence is poised to completely transform space exploration. The following are important areas where AI is having an impact:

- Autonomous Rovers and Landers: AI-driven rovers, like NASA's Perseverance, are capable of navigating terrain, analyzing samples, and making choices in real time without the need for human assistance.

- AI allows spacecraft to process large volumes of data, identify hazards, and change their trajectory without waiting for commands from Earth. This is known as "Deep Space Navigation."

- In order to find exoplanets, spot anomalies, and forecast planetary conditions, artificial intelligence algorithms examine astronomy data.

Space Colonization Driven by AI

AI will be essential to maintaining life in alien environments as humanity attempts to colonize Mars and beyond:

- Autonomous Habitat Construction: Without direct human supervision, robotics powered by AI might put together structures on the Moon or Mars.

- AI in Life Support Systems: To protect astronauts,

intelligent AI systems might keep an eye on temperature, radiation exposure, and oxygen levels.

- In order to create self-sustaining colonies, artificial intelligence (AI) may help with the extraction and utilization of alien resources like minerals and water ice.

Space AI Challenges

Even though AI has enormous potential for space travel, there are still obstacles to overcome:

- Unpredictable Environments: AI needs to be able to adjust to harsh and uncertain situations, like radiation in deep space or dust storms on Mars.
- Ethical Considerations: Governance frameworks must be built to determine the degree of autonomy and decision-making power of AI if it plays a major part in space colonization.

As technology develops, artificial intelligence (AI) could help mankind become an interplanetary species. AI is a vital instrument for increasing human presence in space.

9.3 AI and Smart Cities' Future

Smart City Definition

AI-driven technologies are incorporated into smart cities to maximize infrastructure, boost productivity, and improve urban living standards. These towns use AI to:

- Traffic and Transportation Management: AI-driven traffic control systems optimize traffic flow and alleviate congestion by utilizing real-time data.
- Energy Efficiency: Smart grids employ AI to control the distribution of electricity, cutting expenses and energy waste.
- Public Safety and Surveillance: AI-powered surveillance systems can speed up emergency response times and identify patterns in crime.

The Function of AI in Sustainability and Urban Planning

- Predictive Analytics for City Growth: AI can

influence urban development by analyzing economic and demographic patterns.

- Waste Management Optimization: AI-powered waste collection systems are able to pinpoint regions that need better waste management and optimize pickup routes.

- AI sensors can monitor pollution levels and assist cities in putting air quality improvement strategies into action.

Difficulties and Dangers of AI-Powered Smart Cities

Smart cities using AI promise increased efficiency, however there are concerns as well:

- Privacy Concerns: AI-powered data collecting and surveillance create moral concerns regarding individual privacy.

- The increasing interconnectedness of smart cities makes them vulnerable to cyberattacks that could compromise vital infrastructure.

- Social Inequality: AI-powered smart cities must make sure that everyone benefits from technology instead of making the digital gap worse.

AI has the potential to revolutionize urban living if it is used properly, improving cities' efficiency, sustainability, and ability to adapt to human demands.

9.4 Autonomous AI's Next 50 Years

AI Developments in the Short Term (2025–2035)

- More Advanced AI Assistants: AI will grow increasingly individualized and competent to manage intricate activities like medical diagnosis and legal consulting.
- Advances in Explainable AI: AI systems will become easier to understand, enabling people to comprehend how AI makes decisions.
- Ethical AI rules: To guarantee equitable and responsible use, governments will enact stricter AI rules.

Evolution of AI in the Mid-Term (2035-2050)

- The integration of artificial intelligence (AI) with brain-computer interfaces (BCIs) has the potential to improve cognitive capacities by interacting directly with the human brain.

- Human-Like AI Avatars: AI-enabled virtual entities might be companions, therapists, or coworkers.

- AI in Governance: To increase efficiency, some corporate and governmental decision-making processes may be delegated to AI.

Long-Term AI Forecasts for 2050 and Later

- Artificial Superintelligence (ASI) Emerges: AI outsmarts humans, resulting in previously unheard-of technical breakthroughs.

- The potential for AI and humans to develop cooperative intelligence, functioning as partners rather than rivals, is known as "Human-AI Symbiosis."

- Interstellar AI Exploration: AI-driven probes may investigate far-off galaxies, gathering information for future human space travel.

The Unpredictable AI Future

Even if artificial intelligence will make remarkable strides over the next fifty years, the future is still unclear. The governance, ethical, and societal implications of AI will determine its place in the world. As AI develops further, how it is created and governed will determine whether it can improve human capabilities or upend current systems.

Autonomous AI has a fascinating and complicated future. AI will keep pushing the envelope of what is conceivable, from the search for artificial general intelligence (AGI) to AI-powered space colonization and the development of smart cities. To guarantee that AI works best for humanity in the ensuing decades, this advancement must be supported by a thorough analysis of the ethical, legal, and sociological ramifications.

CHAPTER 10

CONCLUSION: CREATING A FUTURE OF AUTONOMOUS AI

Humanity is at a turning point in determining how artificial intelligence will influence the future as technology continues to advance at a never-before-seen rate. The advancement of autonomous AI has promise for redefining human-machine interactions, revolutionizing industries, and changing daily life. To guarantee that AI's advantages are maximized while its perils are minimized, significant ethical, societal, and governance issues are brought about by this shift.

This chapter examines the need for strong governance and policy frameworks, the delicate balance between human and AI partnership, and the actions necessary to get ready for a society increasingly influenced by autonomous AI. Lastly, it offers an analysis of the long-term effects of AI and the shared accountability required to influence its course.

10.1 The balancing act: cooperation between humans and AI

AI's Function as an Augmenting Force

AI should be seen as a formidable enhancement tool rather than a substitute for human abilities, despite the fact that a large portion of the conversation about AI centers on automation and the possibility of job displacement. The capacity of AI to analyze enormous volumes of data, spot trends, and improve decision-making is its greatest strength. Human judgment, inventiveness, and emotional intelligence, however, are still invaluable.

Human-AI cooperation can flourish in the following important areas:

- Healthcare: Robotic operations and AI-powered diagnostics improve medical accuracy, but doctors and nurses still play a crucial role in patient care, empathy, and decision-making.
- While AI-powered personalized learning

technologies can customize instruction for each student, teachers are still crucial for social-emotional learning, critical thinking development, and mentoring.

- Business and Finance: AI can automate repetitive tasks and monitor market trends, but complicated negotiations, ethical dilemmas, and strategic decision-making require human experience.

Using AI to Increase Human Productivity

In many different industries, autonomous AI systems have the potential to boost productivity. Instead of taking the place of workers, AI can:

- Automate monotonous jobs so that people can concentrate on addressing complicated problems.
- Strengthen research and development through increased innovation.
- Increase workplace productivity by streamlining processes and cutting down on mistakes.

Governments and businesses need to take the initiative

to incorporate AI into the workforce by:

- Employees are being upskilled to use AI tools.
- Promoting transdisciplinary cooperation between domain experts and AI developers.
- Enacting laws that support AI's use as an adjunct to human labor rather than as a replacement for it.

10.2 Autonomous AI Policy and Governance

The necessity of regulatory frameworks

Comprehensive regulatory frameworks are becoming more and more necessary as AI becomes more autonomous. AI has the potential to be abused in ways that are detrimental to people, economies, and societies if it is not properly regulated. Regulatory frameworks ought to cover:

- Fairness and Bias: AI systems need to be transparent and built to reduce bias in judgment.
- Privacy and Data Protection: To prevent the exploitation of users' personal information, AI-driven systems should adhere to strict data

protection regulations.

- Legal frameworks must specify who bears responsibility in the event that AI systems malfunction or injure people.
- Security and Cyber Threats: To avoid any weaknesses, the function of AI in cybersecurity should be closely watched.

International Cooperation on AI Regulation

International collaboration is crucial to creating successful AI governance because AI is a global technology. Policymakers need to collaborate in order to:

- Create international ethics guidelines for AI.
- Prevent a small number of influential organizations from monopolizing AI.
- Make sure AI developments benefit all people, not just a few nations or organizations.

While initiatives like the OECD's AI Principles and the European Union's AI Act are early examples of governance frameworks, international cooperation is required to address AI's long-term effects.

10.3 Getting Ready for an Autonomous AI World

Workforce Readiness and Education

AI has the potential to upend established job markets, necessitating a change in worker training and educational goals. In order to get ready for this change, organizations should:

- Include AI literacy in school curricula to make sure pupils are aware of both the advantages and disadvantages of AI.
- Emphasize abilities like ethical reasoning, critical thinking, and interpersonal communication that are difficult for AI to imitate.
- Encourage lifelong learning to assist employees in adjusting to changes in technology.

Redefining Structures in Economics

Economic policy debates need to change as AI-driven

automation alters job trends. The following are some potential tactics to mitigate AI's economic impact:

- A financial safety net for people displaced by automation is provided by the Universal Basic Income (UBI).
- Reskilling and Job Transition Programs: Putting money into workforce development to assist people in transitioning into jobs that complement AI.
- Tax Policies on AI and Automation: Introducing measures to guarantee the equitable distribution of AI's financial gains.

Social and Ethical Aspects to Take Into Account

As AI permeates more aspects of daily life, society must confront important ethical issues:

- How should moral decision-making be incorporated into AI programming?
- If any, what rights ought to be granted to AI entities?
- How can AI be developed to improve human welfare instead of taking the place of interpersonal

relationships?

To ensure AI serves humanity's best interests, ethicists, engineers, legislators, and the general public must collaborate across disciplinary boundaries to address these issues.

10.4 Concluding Remarks on AI's Contribution to Future Development

The Two-Sided Sword of AI Progress

The advancement of AI has both great promise and serious risks. Ethical development, prudent deployment, and meticulous planning are essential to a future in which AI serves humanity. The outcome will depend on how mankind decides to use the technology, which is neither intrinsically good nor harmful.

Call for Group Accountability

The development of AI is not just up to researchers and legislators; it is a shared duty among:

- Governments: To develop regulations that guarantee AI is applied for the benefit of the general population.
- Businesses: To invest in workforce development and ethically apply AI.
- Educators: To equip the next generation to live in a world powered by artificial intelligence.
- Individuals: To stay informed and participate in conversations regarding the implications of AI.

At a glance

The incorporation of AI into all facets of human life will characterize the upcoming decades. AI has the ability to address some of the most important issues facing the globe, such as disease eradication and climate change, if it is used wisely. But this future won't just happen; it needs to be actively molded by thoughtful consideration, teamwork, and moral dedication.

The decisions made now will shape the civilization of tomorrow as we approach an AI-powered future. In order to create a future where humans and AI coexist peacefully, the task is not to halt AI's advancement but to make sure that development is consistent with human values and goals.

ABOUT THE AUTHOR

 Author and thought leader in the IT field Taylor Royce is well known. He has a two-decade career and is an expert at tech trend analysis and forecasting, which enables a wide audience to understand complicated concepts.

Royce's considerable involvement in the IT industry stemmed from his passion with technology, which he developed during his computer science studies. He has extensive knowledge of the industry because of his experience in both software development and strategic consulting.

Known for his research and lucidity, he has written multiple best-selling books and contributed to esteemed tech periodicals. Translations of Royce's books throughout the world demonstrate his impact.

Royce is a well-known authority on emerging technologies and their effects on society, frequently requested as a speaker at international conferences and as a guest on tech podcasts. He promotes the development of ethical technology, emphasizing problems like data privacy and the digital divide.

In addition, with a focus on sustainable industry growth, Royce mentors upcoming tech experts and supports IT education projects. Taylor Royce is well known for his ability to combine analytical thinking with technical know-how. He sees a time when technology will ethically benefit humanity.

www.ingramcontent.com/pod-product-compliance
Lightning Source LLC
LaVergne TN
LVHW022350060326
832902LV00022B/4367